Semiannual Report to Congress

October 1, 2013 – March 31, 2014
OIG-CA-14-009

Office of Inspector General
Department of the Treasury

Highlights

During this semiannual reporting period, the Office of Audit issued 36 products and the Office of Small Business Lending Fund (SBLF) Program Oversight issued 9 products that identified monetary benefits totaling approximately $161,000. Work by the Office of Investigations resulted in 1 arrest and 22 convictions. Some of our more significant results for the period are described below.

- KPMG LLP, under Office of Inspector General supervision, issued an unmodified opinion on the Department of the Treasury's fiscal year 2013 financial statements. The auditors reported a material weakness related to reporting at the Internal Revenue Service and a significant deficiency related to information systems controls at the Bureau of the Fiscal Service (Fiscal Service).

- The Office of Audit found Fiscal Service's decisions to establish the Direct Express® Debit MasterCard® program and select Comerica Bank (Comerica) as the program's financial agent were reasonable; however, its analyses and documentation of those decisions should have been more complete. Initially, Comerica agreed to provide the debit card services at no cost. Fiscal Service later amended the agreement to pay Comerica $5 for each new enrollment and up to $20 million for infrastructure improvements; Fiscal Service's decision to amend the agreement was not fully supported. In total, Comerica was paid $32.5 million as of June 2013. Fiscal Service has announced a rebid of the financial agent agreement, to be completed by December 2014, and agreed to a number of our recommendations to improve program administration.

- The Office found weak controls over travel spending at the Community Development Financial Institutions Fund. Auditors identified numerous audit exceptions and reported an instance where the Fund's former Director and other Fund personnel incurred unreasonable and unnecessary travel expenditures for a trip to Hawaii.

- The Office also reported that the Gulf Coast Ecosystem Restoration Council (Council) made notable progress towards establishing in Initial Comprehensive Plan; however, the Council did not publish the plan in the *Federal Register* by a mandated deadline. In addition, the Initial Comprehensive Plan as published, did not include all the elements required by the Resources and Ecosystems Sustainability, Tourist Opportunities, and Revived Economies of the Gulf Coast States Act of 2012 (RESTORE Act).

- The Office of SBLF Program Oversight reported that guidance established by Treasury to ensure that lenders participating in the State Small Business Credit Initiative (SSBCI)-funded Capital Access Programs have a meaningful amount of capital-at-risk is at odds with the longstanding operating structure of such programs.

- The Office also reported that 2 years have passed since American Samoa was awarded SSBCI funds, but it has not used the awarded funds to extend credit to small businesses in the territory.

- The Office of Investigations found that a Mint contractor had substantially overcharged the Mint for freight shipping costs through Federal Express. Under a settlement agreement with the U.S. Department of Justice (Justice), the contractor will repay the Mint approximately $530,000. Debarment proceedings against the contractor are in progress.

- The investigation substantiated that a Pennsylvania resident had fraudulently redeemed Treasury bonds totaling approximately $102,000. Under a settlement agreement with Justice, the subject will repay the Fiscal Service the full amount, plus interest.

Message from the Inspector General

I am pleased to present the Treasury Office of Inspector General's Semiannual Report to Congress for the 6-month period ending March 31, 2014. The audits, reviews, and investigations described in this report illustrate our office's commitment to promoting the integrity, efficiency, and effectiveness of Treasury programs and operations under our jurisdictional oversight. In this message I will highlight our office's efforts to oversee two key programs–the Small Business Lending Fund (SBLF) and the State Small Business Credit Initiative (SSBCI). SBLF and SSBCI collectively provided $5.5 billion to spur small business lending and investment.

Our office's strong oversight of SBLF activities helps ensure transparency in how Treasury reports the results of this major small business initiative. After Treasury released a report on SBLF program accomplishments in January 2014 declaring $11.2 billion in lending growth, my office released an important assessment of the program's impact. Our work, which was the first attempt to identify how participants used their SBLF funds, emphasized that the lending growth reported by participants did not constitute new loans and commitments, nor was all of the growth attributable to SBLF funding.

Under SSBCI, each state was allowed to design its own small business support programs to respond to local economic conditions, challenging my staff to learn each new state program. As states accelerated their use of SSBCI funds in 2013, we accelerated our audits of their expenditures. At the end of this reporting period, we completed or had in-progress 14 audits, many of which identified misused funds or conflicts of interest, and the need for more effective oversight by Treasury. Looking forward, our work in this area may continue to increase as the President's fiscal year 2015 request proposes to extend the SSBCI program with an additional $1.5 billion of funding.

In closing, while I have highlighted above the excellent work by our SBLF and SSBCI auditors, I would like to acknowledge the entire Treasury Office of Inspector General staff for the significant audit and investigative results that are summarized in this Semiannual Report.

Eric M. Thorson
Inspector General

Contents

Office of Inspector General Overview

The Department of the Treasury's (Treasury or Department) Office of Inspector General (OIG) was established pursuant to the 1988 amendments to the Inspector General Act of 1978. OIG is headed by an Inspector General appointed by the President, with the advice and consent of the Senate.

OIG performs independent, objective reviews of Treasury programs and operations, except for those of the Internal Revenue Service (IRS) and the Troubled Asset Relief Program (TARP), and keeps the Secretary of the Treasury and Congress fully informed of problems, deficiencies, and the need for corrective action. The Treasury Inspector General for Tax Administration (TIGTA) performs oversight related to IRS. A Special Inspector General and the Government Accountability Office (GAO) perform oversight related to TARP.

OIG has five components: (1) Office of Audit, (2) Office of Investigations, (3) Office of Small Business Lending Fund (SBLF) Program Oversight, (4) Office of Counsel, and (5) Office of Management. OIG is headquartered in Washington, D.C., and has an audit office in Boston, Massachusetts.

The Office of Audit, under the leadership of the Assistant Inspector General for Audit, performs and supervises audits, attestation engagements, and evaluations. The Assistant Inspector General for Audit has two deputies. One is primarily responsible for performance audits and the other is primarily responsible for financial management, information technology (IT), and financial assistance audits.

The Office of Investigations, under the leadership of the Assistant Inspector General for Investigations, performs investigations and conducts initiatives to detect and prevent fraud, waste, and abuse in Treasury programs and operations under our jurisdiction. The Office of Investigations also manages the Treasury OIG Hotline to facilitate reporting of allegations involving Treasury programs and activities.

The Office of SBLF Program Oversight, under the leadership of a Special Deputy Inspector General, conducts, supervises, and coordinates audits and investigations of SBLF and the State Small Business Credit Initiative (SSBCI).

The Office of Counsel, under the leadership of the Counsel to the Inspector General, provides legal advice to the Inspector General and all OIG components. The office represents the OIG in administrative legal proceedings and provides a variety of legal services including (1) processing Freedom of Information Act and *Giglio*[1] requests; (2) conducting ethics training; (3) ensuring compliance with financial disclosure requirements; (4) reviewing proposed legislation and regulations; (5) reviewing administrative subpoena requests; and (6) preparing for the Inspector General's signature, cease and desist letters to be sent to persons and entities misusing the Treasury seal and name.

---

[1] *Giglio* is information that refers to material that may call into question the character or testimony of a prosecution witness in a criminal trial.

The Office of Management, under the leadership of the Assistant Inspector General for Management, provides services to maintain the OIG administrative infrastructure.

OIG's fiscal year 2014 appropriation is $34.8 million. As of March 31, 2014, OIG had 180 full-time staff, 18 of whom work for the Office of SBLF Program Oversight and are funded on a reimbursable basis.

Treasury's Management and Performance Challenges

In accordance with the Reports Consolidation Act of 2000, the Treasury Inspector General annually provides the Secretary of the Treasury with his perspective on the most serious management and performance challenges facing the Department. In a memorandum to Secretary Lew dated November 14, 2013, Inspector General Thorson reported four challenges. All are repeat challenges from last year. The following is a synopsis of the matters included in that memorandum. The Inspector General's annual Management and Performance Challenges Memoranda are available, in their entirety, on the Treasury OIG website.

Continued Implementation of Dodd-Frank (Repeat Challenge)

In our prior year memorandum, we referred to this challenge as "Transformation of Financial Regulation" but renamed it as many aspects of the Dodd-Frank Wall Street Reform and Consumer Protection Act of 2010 (Dodd-Frank) have been implemented and are maturing. This challenge focuses on the responsibilities of Treasury and the Secretary under Dodd-Frank.

Management of Treasury's Authorities Intended to Support and Improve the Economy (Repeat Challenge)

This challenge focuses on the administration of broad authorities given to Treasury by the Congress to address the financial crisis under the Housing and Economic Recovery Act of 2008, the Emergency Economic Stabilization Act of 2008, the American Recovery and Reinvestment Act of 2009 (Recovery Act), and the Small Business Jobs Act of 2010.

Anti-Money Laundering and Terrorist Financing/Bank Secrecy Act Enforcement (Repeat Challenge)

This challenge focuses on the difficulties Treasury faces to ensure criminals and terrorists do not use our financial networks to sustain their operations and/or launch attacks against the U.S.

Gulf Coast Restoration Trust Fund Administration (Repeat Challenge)

This challenge focuses on Treasury's administration of the Gulf Coast Restoration Trust Fund, established by the Resources and Ecosystems Sustainability, Tourist Opportunities, and Revived Economies of the Gulf Coast States Act of 2012 (RESTORE Act) in response to the April 2010 *Deepwater Horizon* oil spill.

Other Areas of Concern

Our memorandum also highlighted three areas of concern—cyber threats, challenges with currency and coin production, and lapses by the Department in maintaining a complete and concurrent record of key activities and decisions.

We also noted challenges faced by the Bureau of the Fiscal Service (Fiscal Service) as it carries out its responsibilities under the Office of Management and Budget (OMB) guidance "Protecting Privacy while Reducing Improper Payments with the Do Not Pay Initiative".

In October 2014, the Inspector General will update the Management and Performance Challenges Memoranda to the Secretary.

Office of Audit – Significant Audits and Other Products

Financial Audits and Attestation Engagements

Treasury's Consolidated Financial Statements

KPMG LLP (KPMG), an independent public accountant working under our supervision, issued an unmodified opinion on the Department's fiscal years 2013 and 2012 consolidated financial statements. The auditor reported a material weakness related to financial reporting at IRS and a significant deficiency related to information systems controls at Fiscal Service. KPMG also reported that the Department's financial management systems did not substantially comply with the requirements of the Federal Financial Management Improvement Act of 1996 related to federal financial management system requirements and applicable federal accounting standards. The audit identified a potential violation of the Anti-Deficiency Act related to voluntary services provided to the Department. **(OIG-14-011)**

In connection with its audit of Treasury's consolidated financial statements, KPMG issued a management letter that identified certain matters involving internal control over financial reporting related to callable capital commitments and custodial revenue transactions, preparing and reviewing financial statement crosswalks, and oversight of a service provider. **(OIG-14-020)**

Other Financial Audits

The Chief Financial Officers Act of 1990, as amended by the Government Management Reform Act of 1994, requires annual financial statement audits of Treasury and any component entities designated by OMB. In this regard, OMB designated IRS for annual financial statement audits. The financial statements of certain other Treasury component entities are audited pursuant to other requirements, their materiality to Treasury's consolidated financial statements, or as a management initiative. The table on the next page shows the audit results for fiscal years 2013 and 2012.

Treasury-audited financial statements and related audits						
	Fiscal year 2013 audit results			Fiscal year 2012 audit results		
Entity	Opinion	Material weaknesses	Significant deficiencies	Opinion	Material weaknesses	Significant deficiencies
Government Management Reform Act/Chief Financial Officers Act requirements						
Department of the Treasury	U	1	1	U	1	1
Internal Revenue Service (A)	U	1	1	U	1	1
Other required audits						
Department of the Treasury's Special-Purpose Financial Statements	U	0	0	U	0	0
Office of Financial Stability (TARP) (A)	U	0	0	U	0	0
Bureau of Engraving and Printing	U	0	1	U	0	1
Community Development Financial Institutions Fund	U	0	0	U	0	0
Office of DC Pensions	(B)	(B)	(B)	U	0	1
Federal Financing Bank	U	0	0	U	0	1
Treasury Forfeiture Fund	U	0	0	U	0	0
Mint						
Financial statements	U	0	0	U	0	0
Custodial gold and silver reserves	U	0	0	U	0	0
Other audited accounts/financial statements that are material to Treasury's financial statements						
Bureau of the Fiscal Service						
Schedule of Federal Debt (A)	U	0	1	U	0	0
Government trust funds	U	0	0	U	0	0
Treasury-managed accounts	U	0	1	U	0	1
Operating cash of the federal government	U	0	1	U	0	1
Exchange Stabilization Fund	U	0	0	U	0	0
Management-initiated audit						
Office of the Comptroller of the Currency	U	0	0	U	0	1
Financial Crimes Enforcement Network	(C)	(C)	(C)	U	0	0
Alcohol and Tobacco Tax and Trade Bureau	U	0	0	U	0	0
U.S. gold reserves held by Federal Reserve Banks	U	0	0	U	0	0

U   Unmodified/unqualified opinion.
(A)   Audited by GAO.
(B)   Audit was in progress as of March 31, 2014.
(C)   Entity was not audited.

The fiscal year 2013 audits of Treasury component entities' financial statements identified the following significant deficiencies. These audits were performed by KPMG or other independent public accountants under our supervision.

- Bureau of Engraving and Printing's controls over monthly inventory account reconciliations. **(OIG-14-021)**
- Fiscal Service's IT controls over systems that it directly managed. **(OIG-14-016, OIG-14-017)**

In connection with the fiscal year 2013 financial statement audits, the auditors issued management letters on other matters involving internal control at the Bureau of Engraving and Printing **(OIG-14-022)**, the Community Development Financial Institutions (CDFI) Fund **(OIG-14-008)** and the Office of the Comptroller of the Currency (OCC) **(OIG-14-025)**. In addition, the auditors issued sensitive but unclassified management reports that provided details of the significant deficiency and recommended corrective actions related to Fiscal Service's IT controls over systems that it directly managed. **(OIG-14-018, OIG-14-019)**

The following instances of noncompliance with the Federal Financial Management Improvement Act of 1996, which all relate to IRS, were reported in connection with the audit of the Department's fiscal year 2013 consolidated financial statements.

Condition	Type of noncompliance
Internal control deficiencies in financial management systems for unpaid tax assessments continue to exist. As a result of these deficiencies, IRS was unable to (1) use its general ledger system and underlying subsidiary records to classify and report federal taxes receivable, compliance assessments, and write-offs for tax transactions, in accordance with federal accounting standards without a labor-intensive manual compensating estimation process; (2) use its subsidiary ledger for unpaid tax assessments to prepare reliable, useful, and timely information to manage and report externally because IRS's classification program does not effectively sort through, identify, and analyze all the relevant transaction information required for proper classification, recording and reporting; and (3) effectively prevent or timely detect and correct errors in recording taxpayer information. (first reported in fiscal year 1997)	Federal financial management systems requirements
Financial management systems were unable to support the taxes receivable amount on the consolidated balance sheet, and the compliance assessments and write-offs in the required supplementary information disclosures, in accordance with *Statement of Federal Financial Accounting Standards No. 7, Accounting for Revenue and Other Financing Sources and Concepts for Reconciling Budgetary and Financial Accounting.* (first reported in fiscal year 1997)	Federal accounting standards

The status of these instances of noncompliance, including progress in implementing remediation plans, will be evaluated as part of the audit of the Department's fiscal year 2014 consolidated financial statements.

Attestation Engagement

KPMG, working under our supervision, issued an unqualified opinion on the Fiscal Service's Trust Fund Management Branch's assertions pertaining to the schedule of assets and liabilities and related schedule of activity of selected trust funds, as of and for the year ended September 30, 2013. The following trust funds were audited.

- Federal Supplementary Medical Insurance Trust Fund

- Federal Hospital Insurance Trust Fund

- Highway Trust Fund

- Airport and Airway Trust Fund

- Hazardous Substance Superfund Trust Fund

- Leaking Underground Storage Tank Trust Fund

- Oil Spill Liability Trust Fund

- Harbor Maintenance Trust Fund

- Inland Waterways Trust Fund

- South Dakota Terrestrial Wildlife Habitat Restoration Trust Fund

The attestation examination did not identify any material weaknesses or significant deficiencies in internal control or instances of reportable noncompliance with laws and regulations. **(OIG-14-005)**

Information Technology Audits and Evaluations

OCC's Network and Systems Security Controls Were Deficient

We performed a series of internal and external vulnerability assessments and penetration tests on OCC's network and systems. We also tested the physical security of OCC's headquarters and performed social engineering tests by using email and phone phishing.[2]

We determined that OCC's security measures were not sufficient to fully prevent and detect unauthorized access into its network and systems by internal threats, or external threats that gained an internal foothold. Also, OCC's security measures were not adequate to fully protect personally identifiable information from internet-based threats. In all, we reported that (1) default usernames and

---

[2] Phishing is a fraud method where the perpetrator uses what appears to be official communication, such as emails or phone calls, in an attempt to gather information from recipients.

passwords were present in OCC's systems, (2) OCC did not fully implement least privilege controls, (3) personally identifiable information on OCC's public-facing web server was vulnerable to unauthorized access, (4) OCC's email servers were vulnerable to spoofed email, (5) OCC's configuration management needs improvement, (6) OCC's Help Desk was susceptible to social engineering attacks, and (7) OCC's patch and version management needs improvement. On a positive note, we found that physical security at OCC's new headquarters location was adequate.

We made 11 recommendations to address these findings. OCC's corrective actions, taken and planned, met the intent of our recommendations. **(OIG-14-001)**

Fiscal Year 2013 Evaluation of Treasury's Federal Information Security Management Act Unclassified Systems

The Federal Information Security Management Act (FISMA) requires each Inspector General to perform an annual, independent evaluation of their agency's information security program and practices. Under a contract monitored by our office, KPMG performed an evaluation of the Department's non-IRS unclassified systems' compliance with FISMA requirements. TIGTA performed the annual FISMA evaluation of the IRS' unclassified systems. Based on the results reported by KPMG and TIGTA, we determined that Treasury's information security program and practices for its unclassified systems are in place and are generally consistent with FISMA. However, the information security program and practices could be more effective.

Specifically, KPMG reported the following at one or more Treasury component entities, excluding IRS.

- Logical account management activities were not in place or not consistently performed (3 component entities).
- Security incidents were not reported timely and under the correct categorization (2 component entities).
- System Security Plans did not follow National Institute of Standards and Technology *Special Publication 800-53, Revision 3, Recommended Security Controls for Federal Information Systems and Organizations* (2 component entities).
- Contingency planning and testing controls were not fully implemented or operating as designed (1 component entity).
- Evidence of successful completion of annual security awareness training was not retained for some users (1 component entity).

In all, KPMG made 11 recommendations to address these control deficiencies. Treasury's Chief Information Officer provided planned corrective actions that met the intent of KPMG's recommendations. **(OIG-CA-14-006)**

Fiscal Year 2013 Evaluation of Treasury's Federal Information Security Management Act Implementation for Its Collateral National Security Systems

KPMG also performed an evaluation, under a contract monitored by our office, of the Department's Collateral National Security Systems' fiscal year 2013 compliance with FISMA requirements. Based on the results reported by KPMG, we determined that Treasury's information security program and practices for the Collateral National Security Systems were in place and generally consistent with FISMA. However, KPMG identified one matter for improvement in the information security program and practices. Treasury's Chief Information Officer provided planned corrective actions that met the intent of the auditors' two recommendations to address the matter. Due to the sensitive nature of these systems, the report is designated sensitive but unclassified. **(OIG-CA-14-005)**

Other Performance Audits and Related Products

Fiscal Service Needs to Improve Program Management of Direct Express

In 2008, Fiscal Service established the Direct Express® Debit MasterCard® program (Direct Express), a program that allowed federal beneficiaries to receive benefit payments electronically using a prepaid debit card. Effective March 2013, individuals, with limited exceptions, could no longer receive federal payments by paper check and would have to either receive the payments by direct deposit to a bank account or through the Direct Express prepaid debit card. We conducted an audit of Direct Express to determine whether Fiscal Service's decision to proceed with the program, selection of the financial agent, and administration of the program were reasonable. As of June 2013, there were approximately 5.5 million enrollees in Direct Express, and Fiscal Service had paid the program's financial agent, Comerica Bank (Comerica), approximately $32.5 million in enrollment fees and infrastructure development support.

We concluded that Fiscal Service's decisions to establish Direct Express and select Comerica as the program's financial agent were reasonable; however, its analyses and documentation of those decisions should have been more complete. In addition, Fiscal Service needs to improve its oversight of Direct Express and administration of the Financial Agency Agreement (FAA).

After conducting a pilot program, Fiscal Service announced in September 2007 that it was seeking applications from financial institutions to serve as the financial agent for Direct Express. A number of institutions responded to the announcement. Fiscal Service decided not to use a cost model or otherwise create a cost estimate to price the program due to the short time to select a financial agent and belief that pricing would be determined by competition. In addition, Fiscal Service did not develop a quality assurance surveillance plan for monitoring the selected financial agent's compliance with the FAA. Although we did not take issue with the selection of Comerica, Fiscal Service could not support its determination that Comerica would provide the lowest cost/highest quality service to the cardholders at the time of its selection. Also, Fiscal Service did not document its evaluation of Comerica's full technical capabilities, including Comerica's stated capacity to process and accommodate a nationwide prepaid debit card program for federal beneficiaries.

Fiscal Service also needs to improve its oversight of Direct Express and administration of the FAA. The agreement, which was effective January 2008, stated that Comerica would not charge any fees to the government. Subsequently, Fiscal Service amended the agreement to compensate Comerica $5 per new enrollment beginning in December 2010 and pay Comerica up to $20 million for infrastructure improvements. Fiscal Service did not fully verify that the improvements were made. Furthermore, revenue and expense information from Comerica was not validated by Fiscal Service. We also noted that paying Comerica for infrastructure development support could provide Comerica with a future competitive advantage in the rebid of the FAA.

In January 2014, Fiscal Service announced a rebid of the Direct Express program's FAA. We noted the solicitation provided a comprehensive description of the program, including the services to be provided and cardholder usage patterns. The solicitation also included a timeline for selection and implementation activities, which are expected to be concluded by December 31, 2014.

We made 13 recommendations to Fiscal Service pertaining to the rebid process and to Direct Express program administration going forward. As examples of the more significant actions needed to improve the program, we recommended that Fiscal Service (1) create an independent estimate to determine whether proposed compensation by bidders is reasonable; (2) include a provision in the FAA requiring notification to OIG of any instances of possible violations of federal criminal laws such as fraud; (3) assess the costs and burden of the program to the cardholders on an ongoing basis as changes to technology and the business environment occur; (4) establish a plan to monitor and document the financial agent's performance under the FAA and take action when requirements are not met; (5) ensure customer feedback from surveys is communicated to the appropriate parties for action, prioritized, and addressed; and (6) ensure that appropriate and complete documentation is maintained for the program. For most recommendations, Fiscal Service has taken or planned corrective actions that met the intent of the recommendations. We have, however, asked Fiscal Service for additional details as to its planned corrective actions for other recommendations. **(OIG-14-031)**

CDFI Fund Needs Better Controls Over Travel

In light of the Administration's broad concerns over prudent use of government funds for travel, in addition to concerns that were raised to our office by a Treasury official with respect to travel by the former Director, we performed an audit of the CDFI Fund's travel expenditures between July 2010 and June 2012.

Overall, we found weak controls at the CDFI Fund to prevent and detect potentially wasteful spending on travel and to ensure compliance with government-wide and departmental travel rules and regulations. Our testing of 130 travel claims by CDFI Fund officials and staff identified audit exceptions in 129 of them (an exception rate of more than 99 percent). These exceptions included unsupported travel claims, unauthorized costs, reimbursement above per diem, costs claimed but not incurred, ineligible expenses, and fees for upgrading to business class. We also identified audit exceptions related to untimely submission of travel claims, inappropriate approvals by undesignated individuals, and missed opportunities for cost savings.

We reported an instance where the former Director, another CDFI Fund official, and two CDFI Fund staff incurred travel expenditures for a trip to Hawaii which were neither reasonable nor necessary given the facts and circumstances surrounding the travel purpose. As a separate matter, we noted during our audit that the Director did not have the express authority to administer the CDFI Fund as a result of the expiration of Treasury Directive (TD) 11-02, *Delegation of Authority for Administering the Community Development Financial Institutions Fund*, in November 2001.

Treasury management agreed with our recommendations to improve controls over processing CDFI Fund travel authorizations and vouchers, but lacked specificity in some of its planned corrective actions with respect to training in travel requirements and the approval process. With regard to audit exceptions identified in specific travel claims, management determined that $3,288 of travel expenses are subject to recovery. Management also addressed the expiration of the Director's authority to administer the CDFI Fund and ratification of Directors' actions since TD 11-02 expired. **(OIG-14-023)**

OCC's Leasing Activities Conformed with Applicable Requirements; Issues with the Former OTS Headquarters Building Need to Be Resolved

We performed an audit of OCC to determine whether its real property leasing policy and procedures complied with applicable laws, rules, and regulations; and to assess whether these policies and procedures were consistently followed. As part of our audit, we reviewed select OCC leases, including its lease for headquarters space at the new Constitution Center in Washington, DC, to assess whether the lease requirements were appropriate. We also reviewed OCC's management and leasing activities related to the former Office of Thrift Supervision (OTS) headquarters property, located at 1700 G Street NW, Washington, DC, which transferred to OCC on July 21, 2011, as provided for in Dodd-Frank.

We concluded that OCC's policies and procedures complied with applicable laws, rules, and regulations. Additionally, OCC consistently followed its established leasing policies and procedures. Furthermore, based on a review of select leases, including the headquarters lease, we found that OCC's lease requirements were appropriate, specifically as to acquiring the appropriate amount of space at a reasonable cost. However, in our review of OCC's leasing authority and activities related to the former OTS headquarters property, we identified a potential issue regarding OCC's absolute rights to the property and its ability to exercise all rights of ownership.

We recommended that OCC review its ownership position of the former OTS headquarters property by performing an analysis and developing a legal opinion of OCC's ownership rights to the property. If OCC determines it holds ownership rights to the former OTS headquarters property, we recommend the bureau take action in an expedient manner to retitle the property in the name of OCC to ensure that its authority, interest, and ownership in the building is uncontestable; or, in the alternative, engage Congress to provide a specific statutory transfer. If OCC determines that it does not hold ownership rights to the former OTS headquarters property, we recommend the bureau coordinate with the General Services Administration to return the property to its inventory.

We also noted two other matters in our report involving the former OTS headquarters property. As the first matter, in a letter dated June 14, 2013, we requested a decision from GAO relating to OCC's authority to retain rental income received from leased space at the former OTS headquarters property, as well as proceeds from any future sale of the property. Accordingly, we recommended OCC implement the actions that GAO determines are necessary from its review of the matter. As the second matter, although OCC is not violating any laws or best practices by being a lessor of the former OTS headquarters property, it is questionable whether the activity correlates with its mission. Therefore, if it is determined that OCC holds ownership rights to the former OTS headquarters property, we recommended that OCC reassess its continued involvement with the property, or whether the property should be sold. OCC's corrective actions, taken and planned, met the intent of our recommendations. **(OIG-14-014)**

Photo of the former OTS headquarters property, located at 1700 G Street, NW, Washington, DC, across the street from the White House complex. The primary tenant of the building is the Consumer Financial Protection Bureau.

Failed Bank Reviews

In 1991, Congress enacted the Federal Deposit Insurance Corporation Improvement Act following the failures of about a thousand banks and thrifts from 1986 to 1990. Among other things, the act added Section 38, Prompt Corrective Action, to the Federal Deposit Insurance Act. Section 38 requires federal banking agencies to take specific supervisory actions in response to certain circumstances.[3]

Section 38 also requires the Inspector General for the primary federal regulator[4] of a failed financial institution to conduct a material loss review (MLR) when the estimated loss to the Deposit Insurance Fund (DIF) is "material." An MLR requires that we determine the causes of the failure and assess the supervision of the institution, including the implementation of the Section 38 Prompt Corrective Action provisions. Section 38, as amended by Dodd-Frank, defines a material loss as a loss to the DIF that exceeds $150 million for 2013, and $50 million in 2014 and thereafter, with a provision for increasing the threshold to $75 million under certain circumstances. Section 38 also requires a review of all bank failures with losses under those threshold amounts for the purposes of (1) ascertaining the grounds identified by OCC for appointing the Federal Deposit Insurance Corporation (FDIC) as receiver, and (2) determining whether any unusual circumstances exist that might warrant a more in-depth review of the loss. This provision applies to bank failures from October 1, 2009, forward.[5]

From the beginning of the recent economic crisis in 2007 through March 2014, FDIC and other banking regulators closed 495 banks and thrifts. Treasury, through OCC and the former OTS, was responsible for regulating 134 of those institutions. Of the 134 failures, 55 resulted in a material loss to the DIF, of which 54 were completed in prior semiannual reporting periods. One MLR was in progress at the end of the semiannual reporting period. There were no new failures of Treasury-regulated banks that required an MLR during this semiannual reporting period. During this period, we completed one in-depth review, Second Federal Savings and Loan Association of Chicago (discussed below), and one review of a failed Treasury-regulated bank that did not meet the material loss threshold as defined in Dodd-Frank, Mountain National Bank, Sevierville, Tennessee (Estimated Loss to the DIF - $33.5 million) **(OIG-14-013)**.

---

[3] Prompt corrective action is a framework of supervisory actions for insured institutions that are not adequately capitalized. It was intended to ensure that action is taken when an institution becomes financially troubled in order to prevent a failure or minimize resulting losses. These actions become increasingly more severe as the institution falls into lower capital categories. The capital categories are well-capitalized, adequately capitalized, undercapitalized, significantly undercapitalized, and critically undercapitalized.

[4] Within Treasury, OCC is the regulator for national banks. Effective July 21, 2011, OCC assumed the regulatory responsibility for federal savings associations that were previously regulated by the former OTS.

[5] Prior to Dodd-Frank, an MLR was required if loss to the DIF from a bank failure exceeded the greater of $25 million or 2 percent of the institution's total assets. There was also no requirement for us to review bank failures with losses less than this threshold.

In-Depth Review of Second Federal Savings and Loan Association of Chicago (Closed July 20, 2012; Estimated Loss to the DIF - $76.9 million)

OCC closed Second Federal Savings and Loan Association of Chicago, Chicago, Illinois, and appointed FDIC as receiver on July 20, 2012. Because the loss estimate was less than the threshold requiring an MLR, we conducted a limited review of the bank that focused on the causes of its failure.[6] During the limited review, we determined that an in-depth review of the bank's failure was warranted based on what we found to be an unusual circumstance—the nature of the bank's unsafe and unsound lending practices, particularly as it related to borrowers with individual taxpayer identification numbers (ITIN). IRS issues ITINs to help individuals comply with the U.S. tax laws, and to provide a means to process and account for tax returns and payments from those not eligible for social security numbers. Before its failure, the bank had originated and purchased a large volume of ITIN loans that resulted in a significant concentration of core capital and allowance for loan and lease losses.

We determined that the OCC *Comptroller's Handbook* did not include guidance on the risks of ITIN lending and was outdated in other high-risk lending areas such as subprime lending and nontraditional mortgages. We recommended that OCC incorporate such guidance in the handbook as appropriate. OCC's corrective actions, taken and planned, met the intent of our recommendations. **(OIG-14-002)**

FinCEN's BSA IT Modernization Program Is on Budget, on Schedule, and Close to Completion

To improve the collection, analysis, and sharing of Bank Secrecy Act (BSA) data, the Financial Crimes Enforcement Network (FinCEN) began a system development effort in November 2006 referred to as the BSA IT Modernization Program (BSA IT Mod). The intent of the effort is, among other things, to transition BSA data from the IRS to FinCEN. BSA IT Mod is estimated to cost $120 million and is to be completed in April 2014. Pursuant to a Congressional directive,[7] we are performing a series of audits of BSA IT Mod to determine if FinCEN is (1) meeting cost, schedule, and performance benchmarks for the program and (2) providing appropriate oversight of contractors. We also assessed any deviations from FinCEN's plan. The period covered by our latest audit was July through December 2013.

As of December 2013, BSA IT Mod remained within budgeted costs and was on schedule to be completed by April 2014. During this audit period, FinCEN completed the first phase of Release 2 of the Broker Information Exchange, the final milestone project, within budget but 7 weeks beyond the planned schedule. We did not consider this delay as significant.

---

[6] *Safety and Soundness: Failed Bank Review of Second Federal Savings and Loan Association of Chicago*, OIG-13-028 (Dec. 20, 2012)

[7] House Report 112-331 directed our office to report on BSA IT Mod, including contractor oversight and progress regarding budget and schedule, every 6 months. This is our fifth report in the series.

Prior to this audit, users told us that there was no mechanism to allow agency BSA IT Mod administrators to monitor staff use of FinCEN Query or to limit access to particular features to detect potential misuse and help ensure that BSA data is safeguarded. Since then, FinCEN has (1) agreed to provide one user agency with logs detailing its employees' use of FinCEN Query, (2) acknowledged its responsibility to monitor usage of FinCEN Query, and (3) begun to develop its own inspection program to monitor potential misuse.

In September 2013, we reported that FinCEN maintained oversight of BSA IT Mod and that program contractors were providing less support to FinCEN's BSA IT Mod program management as the development effort moved into operations and maintenance. We also found that Treasury's Office of the Chief Information Officer monitoring of the program was appropriate based on the overall positive track record by FinCEN managing the BSA IT Mod development effort. During this audit period, FinCEN's oversight responsibilities increased. It provided more direction and oversight of the integration across the various contracts, as contractors transitioned away from providing development program support. No change occurred in the level of program oversight by the office.

We recommended that FinCEN (1) continue to work with users to address user requests for training and enhancements and (2) make agencies aware of the process for contacting FinCEN if misuse of BSA data is suspected. FinCEN's corrective actions, taken and planned, met the intent of our recommendations. **(OIG-14-029)**

Transfer of OTS Functions Is Completed

During this semiannual period, our office, together with FDIC and the Board of Governors of the Federal Reserve System (FRB) and Consumer Financial Protection Bureau OIGs, issued the seventh and final joint review of the transfer, pursuant to Title III of the Dodd-Frank, of the functions, employees, funds, and property of the former OTS to FRB, FDIC, and OCC. In accordance with Title III, the transfer occurred in July 2011.

During our first review, we determined the Joint Implementation Plan (Plan) for the transfer prepared by the FRB, FDIC, OCC, and OTS generally conformed to relevant Title III provisions. Since then, we have reported every 6 months on the status of the Plan's implementation. In prior reports on the Plan implementation, we determined that the Plan has been implemented for the most part, as the functions, people, and property of OTS were transferred to FRB, FDIC, and OCC in accordance with Title III and the Plan. We also reported that procedures and safeguards were in place at FDIC and OCC as outlined in the Plan to ensure that transferred employees are not unfairly disadvantaged, a key requirement in Title III.

In our final review, we determined that both FDIC and OCC complied with the act by providing the protections afforded to the transferred OTS employees for the required 30-month period following the transfer. Accordingly, we did not make any recommendations. **(OIG-14-030)**

Audit of New Mexico Mortgage Finance Authority's Payment Under 1602 Program

Under the Treasury's 1602 Program—*Payments to States for Low-Income Housing Projects in Lieu of Low-Income Housing Credits for 2009*—authorized by section 1602 of the Recovery Act, state housing credit agencies were allowed to exchange a portion of their low-income housing credits for Program funds to be disbursed to eligible subawardees to help finance either the construction or the acquisition and rehabilitation of qualified low-income housing projects. As part of our ongoing oversight of the program, we are conducting audits of awards made to selected state housing credit agencies to assess whether the agencies awarded 1602 Program funds complied with the program's requirements contained in Treasury's terms and conditions of award.

In the case of the New Mexico Mortgage Finance Authority (MFA), we found that MFA complied with the 1602 Program requirements for receiving its $47.8 million of program funds as well as requirements for subawarding those funds to low-income housing projects. As required by the 1602 Program, MFA established a process for monitoring the long-term viability of projects and their compliance with program requirements, and met all of Treasury's reporting requirements. Based on our review of MFA's administration and oversight activities, we concluded that the projects funded with 1602 Program funds met the subaward requirements. In our report, we cautioned that MFA must continue to ensure compliance with the terms and conditions over the remaining 15-year compliance period. We did not make any recommendations to Treasury. **(OIG-14-028)**

RESTORE Act Oversight

Gulf Coast Ecosystem Restoration Council Faces Challenges in Completing Initial Comprehensive Plan

Congress passed the RESTORE Act in response to the April 2010 *Deepwater Horizon* oil spill. The act established the Gulf Coast Ecosystem Restoration Council (Council). The Council was required to publish an Initial Comprehensive Plan no later than July 6, 2013, that incorporated the strategy, projects, and programs recommended by the President's Gulf Coast Restoration Task Force to restore the Gulf Coast's ecosystem.

We reported in October 2013 that while the Council made notable progress towards establishing the Initial Comprehensive Plan, the Council did not publish the plan in the *Federal Register* by the mandated deadline. In addition, the Initial Comprehensive Plan as published did not include all the elements required by the RESTORE Act. Instead, the Council plans to include all required elements in future versions of the Comprehensive Plan. We acknowledged in our report the necessity for the Council to move cautiously in establishing the Initial Comprehensive Plan due to the (1) uncertainty of the amount that will eventually be deposited into the Gulf Coast Restoration Trust Fund,

(2) complexity of developing a plan of this scope, (3) multiple stakeholders involved in the process, and (4) coordination required with other Gulf Coast region assessment and restoration efforts.[8]

We recommended that the Chairperson of the Council ensure that timelines are established as soon as practicable for the next steps listed in the *Draft Initial Comprehensive Plan: Restoring the Gulf Coast's Ecosystem and Economy* (Draft Initial Comprehensive Plan) to include (1) refining objectives and evaluation criteria; (2) establishing advisory committees as determined necessary; (3) developing regulations establishing the oil spill restoration impact allocation formula; (4) releasing a schedule for the submission of proposals from Council members; (5) selecting and publishing a Funded Priorities List; and (6) adopting a 10-Year Funding Strategy. We also recommended that the Chairperson of the Council continue to work with Council members towards developing the Comprehensive Plan to include all elements required by the RESTORE Act. The Council's corrective actions taken and planned met the intent of our recommendations. **(OIG-14-003)**

Other Products

Referrals of Potential OFAC Violations by Three Banks

During our ongoing audit of FinCEN's and the Office of Foreign Assets Control's (OFAC) use of blocked transaction reports for suspicious activity reporting, we identified 387 suspicious activity reports describing transactions processed by three filing financial institutions that potentially violated the OFAC sanctions program. The suspicious activity reports described either (1) transactions that were initially blocked or rejected but then were resent with the suspicious terms omitted or altered and were then processed by the bank or (2) instances in which the bank blocked or rejected transactions but processed other similar, or almost identical, related transactions. We referred these potential violations to OFAC and OCC, respectively, for appropriate enforcement action. Due to the sensitive nature of information in suspicious activity reports, these referrals are designated sensitive but unclassified. **(OIG-CA-14-001, OIG-CA-14-002)**

---

[8] The Council published the Draft Initial Comprehensive Plan for comment in the Federal Register on May 29, 2013. It unanimously approved the Initial Comprehensive Plan on August 28, 2013, after completion of our fieldwork.

Office of SBLF Program Oversight – Significant Audits

State Small Business Credit Initiative

The Small Business Jobs Act of 2010 established the SSBCI program, which awarded $1.5 billion to states, territories, and eligible municipalities to support state programs that lend to and invest in small businesses. Under the initiative, participating states use the federal funds for programs that leverage private lending to help finance small businesses and manufacturers that are creditworthy, but are not getting the loans they need to expand and create jobs. SSBCI builds on new and existing models for state small business programs, including those that finance loan loss reserves and provide loan insurance, loan guarantees, venture capital funds, and collateral support. To date, Treasury has disbursed approximately $1 billion of the funds awarded under the program to 57 states, territories, and municipalities that are participating in SSBCI. Recipients must report quarterly and annually on their use of the funds.

The act also created within Treasury OIG the Office of SBLF Program Oversight. This office is responsible for identifying instances of intentional or reckless misuse of SSBCI funds. Program funds are disbursed in three allotments and are subject to being withheld pending the results of an audit by the office. During this semiannual reporting period, the office completed eight audits on states' use of federal funds.

Treasury Needs to Modify Its Capital-at-Risk Requirements for Capital Access Programs

Guidance established by Treasury to ensure that lenders participating in SSBCI-funded Capital Access Programs (CAP) have a meaningful amount of capital-at-risk is at odds with the longstanding operating structure of such programs. The Small Business Jobs Act authorizing the SSBCI program requires that a lender filing a loan for enrollment in a state CAP have a meaningful amount of its own capital resources at risk in the loan. According to Treasury's *SSBCI Policy Guidelines*, the "meaningful amount" requirement is met when a private lender bears 20 percent or more of the loss from a loan default.

However, over the past 20 years CAPs have operated as portfolio insurance programs. When a participating lender originates a loan, the lender and borrower combine to contribute a percentage of the loan or line of credit, from 2 percent to 7 percent, into a CAP reserve fund held by the lender. The lender's aggregate CAP reserve fund is built through the accumulation of premiums paid by the lender, borrower, and state, and can be used to recover 100 percent of a lender's losses on any loan. In many instances, lenders may have sufficient CAP reserves to cover 100 percent of a loan default. While the reserve fund is available as cash collateral to cover losses on all loans in a lender's CAP portfolio, the lender's percentage contribution to the fund for an individual loan is limited from 2 percent to 7 percent of the defaulted loan value. Based on a strict application of the current *SSBCI Policy Guidelines*, the lender's at-risk capital would be deemed non-compliant, as the percentage of the lender's at-risk capital would be lower than the 20 percent it is required to bear in the case of a loan default. Moreover, Treasury's capital-at-risk requirement would be satisfied only when the balance of a lender's aggregate CAP reserve fund was 80 percent or less of the defaulted SSBCI loan balance.

Additionally, some states allow lenders to use payments from subsequently enrolled loans to pay prior losses when lenders deplete their reserves. Thus, lenders may recover 100 percent of their losses even when their reserve funds are insufficient to cover the losses at the time the loan defaults. Treasury acknowledged that CAPs traditionally operate in this manner to help lenders when there is an early loss that wipes out their reserve funds. It also provides an incentive for lenders to continue enrolling new loans, making CAPs appealing to prospective SSBCI lenders.

The SSBCI Program Director acknowledged that applying the capital-at-risk requirement on a loan basis with a 20-percent capital-at-risk threshold, as required in the *SSBCI Policy Guidelines*, is inconsistent with the standard operational design of CAPs. Doing so could also reduce the marketability of CAPs and their effectiveness within SSBCI.

We recommended that the Deputy Assistant Secretary for Small Business, Housing, and Community Development revise the *SSBCI Policy Guidelines* to (1) redefine how the capital-at-risk requirement should be applied within the context of the traditional operational design of CAPs, and (2) specify whether lenders may use subsequent premium payments to cover past losses. Treasury's planned corrective actions met the intent of our recommendations. **(OIG-SBLF-14-001)**

American Samoa's Administrative Expenses and Reporting

American Samoa may not be fully positioned to provide credit support to small businesses and has continued to violate key terms of its Allocation Agreement. Although 2 years have passed since the territory of American Samoa was awarded SSBCI funds, it has used none of the awarded funds to extend credit to small businesses in the territory. The territory also has not provided Treasury with records that would allow the Department to determine whether the territory is "fully positioned" to provide credit support to small businesses, as required by its Allocation Agreement. Moreover, American Samoa continues to violate key terms of its Allocation Agreement as it: (1) did not obtain Treasury's prior approval for three changes to the entity designated to administer the SSBCI funds; (2) did not submit two of its quarterly reports or its 2012 Annual Report to Treasury on time, causing Treasury to declare a general event of default of American Samoa's Allocation Agreement; and (3) incorrectly certified or did not certify the accuracy of several of its quarterly reports. Despite these factors, Treasury has been slow to hold American Samoa accountable for its noncompliance and to render a decision as to whether to reduce, suspend, or terminate future disbursements. Finally, we identified $49,155 in unsupported personnel and travel expenses that should be disallowed and excluded from "funds used" that the territory claims in its future quarterly reports.

We recommended Treasury immediately determine whether American Samoa has again defaulted on its Allocation Agreement. We also recommended that if the territory has defaulted on its agreement and has not remedied the default, Treasury should determine whether a reduction, suspension, or termination of future funding to the territory is warranted. If American Samoa's SSBCI funding is not terminated, the territory should first be required to comply with the terms of its Allocation Agreement, and Treasury should approve the agreement modifications before disbursing additional funds. Finally, Treasury should disallow the $49,155 in personnel and travel costs identified by the audit. Treasury's planned corrected actions met the intent of our recommendations. **(OIG-SBLF-14-007)**

North Carolina's Use of Federal Funds for Capital Access and Other Credit Support Programs

The state of North Carolina appropriately used most of the $4.9 million in SSBCI funds it had obligated or expended, but contributed $6,690 to a reserve fund under the CAP to refinance one loan prohibited by the Act. Because Treasury, through the *National Standards*, does not require participating states to verify the accuracy of lender representations as to the nature and compliance of loans, we did not find the misuse to be "reckless" or "intentional." Upon learning the loan was prohibited, North Carolina requested that the lender return the SSBCI funds and remove the matching borrower and lender fees from its reserve account.

Additionally, North Carolina did not fully comply with the certification requirement for sex offender assurances for 19 of the 45 transactions tested as required in the Act, *SSBCI Policy Guidelines*, and *National Standards*. Despite the inadequate assurances, the state certified for June 2012, September 2012, December 2012, March 2013, and June 2013, that it was in compliance with all SSBCI requirements, which was materially inaccurate. Additionally, North Carolina inaccurately reported to Treasury the total amount of an enrolled investment on three separate occasions because it misreported the private investor's contribution to the investment. These errors occurred because fund managers reported preliminary numbers from investment documents before receiving the final executed agreements. The SSBCI funds invested were reported accurately, but misreporting total funding can distort critical program performance indicators. Both the materially inaccurate compliance certifications and misreported total investment can trigger an event(s) of default of North Carolina's SSBCI Allocation Agreement with Treasury.

North Carolina also reported $10.3 million in Venture Capital commitments with SSBCI funds to four Angel investment funds as obligated funds even though only $2.9 million had been pledged to investees. Angel Funds comprise a group or network of investors that pool their investment capital; and it can take months, even years, to identify and commit funds to specific investees. Treasury considers capital commitments to Angel Funds as obligated funds, however, we are concerned that the method of reporting capital commitments as obligated before specific investees are identified may misrepresent the amount of funds a state has used and inflate program accomplishments. Moreover, this reporting practice allows states to prematurely qualify for successive funding disbursements before committing capital to investees and is inconsistent with Treasury's guidance for annually reporting leverage ratios.

We recommended that Treasury verify that the state has withdrawn the $6,690 in SSBCI support from the refinanced loan and reimbursed the SSBCI account for its contribution. We also recommended that Treasury determine whether a general event of default has occurred of the state's Allocation Agreement, and if so, take appropriate action. Further, we recommended that Treasury revise the definition of funds obligated for Venture Capital programs to include only those that have been designated for specific investees, and require participants to distinguish Venture Capital funds obligated to Angel Funds and not yet disbursed to investees from other obligated funds when submitting quarterly reports. Finally, we recommended that Treasury adopt a standard definition for "funds used" for all program reporting purposes. Treasury's planned corrective actions met the intent of our recommendations. **(OIG-SBLF-14-009)**

Illinois' Use of Federal Funds for Capital Access and Other Credit Support Programs

The state of Illinois appropriately used most of the $34.5 million in SSBCI funds it had expended as of March 31, 2013, but spent $105,000 to participate in a loan that was used to purchase the stock of a company representing its entire ownership interest, which is prohibited by *SSBCI Policy Guidelines*. The transaction constituted a reckless misuse of funds because Illinois officials should have known that such use was prohibited, and the state did not exercise ordinary care in ascertaining how the loan proceeds would be used despite evidence in the loan file that the borrower intended to purchase stock of a company. State officials also did not investigate representations made by the borrower and lender that contradicted loan documents.

Additionally, 22 other transactions did not fully comply with lender sex offender certification requirements. Illinois, acting in the capacity of a direct lender or investor, neglected to execute lender certifications on the state's behalf as prescribed in the *National Standards*. Despite the inadequate assurances, Illinois certified for June 2012, September 2012, December 2012, and March 2013, that it was in compliance with all SSBCI requirements, which was materially inaccurate. Finally, in its 2012 Annual Report, Illinois unintentionally overstated by $4.7 million the amount of private financing associated with one loan because the financing structure of the transaction was changed without the state's knowledge.

We recommended that Treasury recoup the $105,000 in recklessly misused funds, notify the state that it has incurred a specific event of default per its Allocation Agreement as a result of the reckless misuse, and require Illinois to modify its Master Agreements with lenders to require that lenders notify the state of any changes in the sex offender status of its principals. We also recommended that Treasury notify Illinois that it must provide lender certifications on its own behalf when acting as a direct lender or investor, and adjust its next Annual Report to correct for the $4.7 million overstatement of a loan participation transaction. Finally, Treasury should determine whether Illinois is in general default of its SSBCI Allocation Agreement due to its failure to comply with lender certification requirements, materially inaccurate compliance certifications, and inaccurate reporting of private financing. Treasury's planned corrective actions met the intent of our recommendations. **(OIG-SBLF-14-005)**

South Carolina's Use of Federal Funds for Capital Access and Other Credit Support Programs

The state of South Carolina appropriately used most of the $16.4 million in SSBCI funds it had expended as of June 30, 2013, but misused $427,500 to participate in a loan that was used to finance the building of a new church sanctuary and make renovations to the existing sanctuary, which is prohibited by *SSBCI Policy Guidelines*. The misuse is not reckless or intentional because *SSBCI Policy Guidelines* do not explicitly prohibit the use of SSBCI funds for non-secular purposes. The state relied on a reasonable interpretation of Treasury's guidance and when it learned the use was prohibited, it self-reported the transaction to Treasury and un-enrolled the loan from the SSBCI program.

We also identified eight other transactions that did not comply with the *National Standards* because the state did not verify that the borrower and lender assurances were complete prior to the transfer of funds. Despite the inadequate assurances, the state certified for June 2012, September 2012, December 2012, March 2013, and June 2013, that it was in compliance with all SSBCI requirements, which was inaccurate.

We recommended that Treasury revise the *SSBCI Policy Guidelines* to clearly state that a business purpose excludes transactions with a non-secular identity, and determine whether South Carolina is in general default of its SSBCI Allocation Agreement for not complying with borrower and lender assurance requirements. Treasury's planned corrective actions met the intent of our recommendations. **(OIG-SBLF-14-006)**

Florida's Use of Federal Funds for Capital Access and Other Credit Support Programs

The state of Florida appropriately used most of the SSBCI funds it had expended or obligated as of December 31, 2012, and complied with program requirements when funding 23 of the 24 transactions we tested. However, the state participated in a $34.7 million Florida Venture Capital Program investment that exceeded the $20 million restriction imposed by the Act on the amount of credit support that can be extended to an investee. Treasury's *SSBCI Policy Guidelines*, which extend the credit restriction to investments, do not specifically address how the credit support restriction should be applied when the investment involves multiple equity instruments. For this reason, we did not find Florida's investment to constitute a misuse of funds. Nevertheless, in the absence of clear guidance, the state should have sought clarification from Treasury prior to making the investment.

Also, Florida overstated administrative expenses in its quarterly reports to Treasury by approximately $55,000. The overstatements occurred as a result of incorrect selection criteria used to pull administrative cost information from the state's accounting system. The state identified and reported the overstatement to Treasury, and Treasury allowed Florida to make the necessary adjustments to its quarterly reports to correct its error. Our review of the adjusted quarterly reports confirmed that the correct amounts were reported.

Additionally, in its June 30, 2012, September 30, 2012, and December 31, 2012, quarterly reports the state overstated by approximately $23 million the amount of SSBCI funds that had been obligated because it included Florida Venture Capital Program reserves that were set aside for future follow-on investments to existing investees. Subsequent to submitting the reports, Treasury informed Florida that the reserve commitments did not meet Treasury's criteria for designating the funds as obligated because the commitments were not firm. At Treasury's direction, Florida removed the reserve funds from the state's reported program activity.

We recommended that Treasury revise its guidelines to clarify how the $20 million credit support restriction should be applied when an investment involves multiple equity instruments. We also recommended that Treasury determine whether there has been a general event of default under Florida's Allocation Agreement resulting from the state's inaccurate reporting of obligated funds. If such an event has occurred and has not been adequately cured, Treasury should determine whether it warrants a reduction, suspension, or termination of future funding to the state. Treasury's corrective actions taken and planned met the intent of our recommendations. **(OIG-SBLF-14-002)**

Louisiana's Eligibility for Its Second Transfer of Funds and the Allowability of Reported Administrative Expenses

The state of Louisiana accurately reported its use of SSBCI funds on the 16 loans and investments we tested and, according to the *SSBCI Policy Guidelines*, was eligible to receive its second disbursement. Additionally, administrative costs charged to the SSBCI program by the state as of December 31, 2012, were reasonable, allowable, and allocable. Because Louisiana complied with the SSBCI program requirements, we made no recommendations. **(OIG-SBLF-14-003)**

West Virginia's Use of Federal Funds for Other Credit Support Programs

The state of West Virginia appropriately used $9.5 million in SSBCI funds on the 28 loans and investments we tested and accurately reported its program activity to Treasury. Additionally, the state's administrative costs charged to the SSBCI program as of June 30, 2013, were reasonable, allowable, and allocable. Because West Virginia complied with the SSBCI program requirements, we made no recommendations. **(OIG-SBLF-14-004)**

Small Business Lending Fund

The Small Business Jobs Act of 2010 also established the SBLF program. The SBLF program was created to provide capital to small banks, with incentives for those banks to increase small business lending. Treasury disbursed more than $4 billion to 332 financial institutions across the country, of which 137 were institutions that used their SBLF investment to refinance securities issued under TARP. The 137 TARP banks received two-thirds of the $4 billion invested in participating banks. Institutions receiving investments under the SBLF program are expected to pay dividends to Treasury at rates that will decrease as the amount of their qualified small business lending increases. Under Section 4107(a) of the act, the Special Deputy Inspector General for SBLF Program Oversight is responsible for audit and investigations related to the SBLF program and must report at least twice a year to the Secretary and the Congress on the results of oversight activities involving the program. During this semiannual reporting period, the Office of SBLF Program Oversight completed one audit of the SBLF program.

Survey of SBLF Participants' Use of Program Funds, Repayment Plans, and Satisfaction with Treasury's Program Administration

We surveyed 325 of the 332 financial institutions participating in the SBLF program to (1) identify how recipient institutions used funds awarded under the program and the factors that most influenced their use of funds, (2) determine participants' plans to repay Treasury's investment and exit the program, and (3) evaluate Treasury's administration of the program. Of the 323 institutions that responded to the survey, 94 percent reported using some portion of their SBLF capital to extend credit to small businesses, and 6 percent reported using all of their SBLF capital for other purposes. Two hundred eighty respondents whom collectively received $3.3 billion were able to quantify how much of the SBLF capital received supported small business lending. These respondents estimated that $1.8 billion went for small business lending and $1.5 billion was used for other purposes, including paying dividends, redeeming equity or debt, or increasing other types of lending.

Respondents were also asked to estimate the percentage of small business lending gains (i.e., growth in lending) that they had reported to Treasury as attributable to the SBLF capital. The 142 participants who gave estimates reported that $1.4 billion (or 58 percent) of the $2.4 billion they collectively reported as small business lending gains between the date of Treasury's investment and March 31, 2013, was a direct result of the SBLF funds. Additionally, because lending gains represent just the difference in outstanding loan principal on a bank's books between two time periods, and are impacted by loan payoffs, we asked respondents to identify the amount of new loans and credit commitments associated with their SBLF capital. About 98 percent of all survey respondents reported an aggregate amount of approximately $22.8 billion in new small business lending, with former TARP banks reporting the same level of new lending activity as that of non-TARP banks, even though they received less SBLF capital. However, respondents differ in how they calculate the amount of new loans and commitments they report to Treasury because Treasury has not clearly defined what is to be reported.

Respondents reported that the demand for certain types of loans, sufficient loan margins, and the capital needs of their banks were the predominant factors that influenced how they used their SBLF funds. Additionally, the ability to receive a lower dividend rate with increased small business lending drove participants to use their SBLF funds on small business loans.

Most of the respondents surveyed plan to repay Treasury's investment and exit the program when the variable dividend rate becomes fixed, or when cheaper capital is available. Finally, over 89 percent of respondents were satisfied overall with Treasury's administration of the SBLF program. However, 52 percent of the respondents who rated their satisfaction with the process reported that they were unsatisfied with Treasury's handling of program fees and penalties.

We recommended and Treasury agreed to establish a clear definition of new loans and commitments to small businesses before administering the next Annual SBLF Lending Survey. Treasury has taken corrective action that met the intent of our recommendation. (**OIG-SBLF-14-008**)

Office of Investigations - Significant Investigations

Mint Contractor Agrees to Pay Approximately $530,000 in Settlement for Overcharging

Our office investigated an allegation that a Mint contractor had substantially overcharged the Mint for freight shipping costs through Federal Express. Extensive review of relevant documents, including some received in compliance with a subpoena, substantiated the allegation. Under a settlement agreement with the U.S. Department of Justice (Justice), the contractor is to repay the Mint approximately $530,000. Debarment proceedings against the contractor are in progress.

Individual Agrees to Pay Approximately $122,000 in Settlement for the Fraudulent Redemption of Treasury Bonds

Fiscal Service reported to our office that a Pennsylvania resident had fraudulently redeemed Treasury bonds totaling approximately $102,000. Our investigation substantiated that the subject had redeemed both his original bonds and a substitute issue of the bonds obtained through a false claim. Under a settlement agreement with Justice, the subject is to repay Fiscal Service the full amount, plus interest.

Individual Convicted for Theft of Government Money

A joint investigation with the Social Security Administration OIG and the U.S. Marshals Service revealed that a citizen had received and negotiated Social Security Administration benefit payments that had continued to be issued in her mother's name for 6 years following her mother's death. The subject pled guilty to one charge, Theft of Government Money, and received a sentence of 18 months of incarceration, 36 months of probation, and approximately $50,000 in restitution.

Lead Analyst Resigns Over Cocaine Use and False Statements

Following an initial allegation that a background check on a GS-15 Lead Analyst in Departmental Offices revealed that he had been charged criminally for the purchase of cocaine, our office investigated the subject and determined he had both purchased cocaine and submitted false and misleading information on his *Electronic Questionnaires for Investigations Processes* application for a security clearance renewal. The false information pertained to the dates of the subject's cocaine use, dates of his arrest and arraignment for the possession of cocaine, and failure to report numerous instances of foreign travel. Justice did not accept the case for criminal prosecution; the subject resigned before administrative action could be taken.

Mint Police Lieutenant Receives Demotion and 90-Day Suspension for Providing False Statements

Our office received an allegation that a Mint Police lieutenant provided false information to a Mint Police detective during the course of an internal investigation. Although the lieutenant claimed to have attempted for 2 hours to contact a replacement so that he could leave his shift early, our investigation substantiated the allegation that the subject left his post unattended to conduct personal business without notifying, or attempting to notify, a supervisor. Justice did not accept the case for criminal prosecution; the Mint Police disciplined the subject with a demotion from lieutenant to senior patrol officer and a 90-day unpaid suspension.

OCC Employee Receives 30-Day Suspension for Exposing Himself Online

We received a complaint that an OCC employee was posing as a 15-year-old male on a social networking site geared toward high school students. Our investigation revealed that the employee had provided a false birthdate when creating his account on the website, and that he had exposed his genitals during live web camera interactions with other users on two occasions. However, because the website did not capture information from the accounts of the users with whom the subject had interacted, no victims could be identified, nor could it be established whether the subject had exposed himself to a minor. When interviewed, the subject admitted that he had exposed himself online, but stated that he did not believe that the users to whom he had exposed himself were minors. The evidence was not sufficient to present the matter to Justice for criminal prosecution, but the subject was given a 30-day unpaid suspension by OCC.

GS-15 Supervisor Retires After Confessing to Viewing Pornography on Office Equipment

During an investigation into an allegation that a GS-15 supervisor at Fiscal Service misused workplace electronics to view pornography, the supervisor admitted to using his office-issued tablet and notebook computer to access websites that offered adult entertainment and escort services during non-work hours. The supervisor retired before administrative disciplinary action could be taken.

Bank Examiner Resigns Over Travel Expense Fraud

An OCC bank examiner was found to have spent almost 2 years submitting approximately $6,000 in fraudulent receipts and travel vouchers to collect "compensation" to which he was not entitled. The case was not accepted for criminal prosecution; the employee resigned before administrative disciplinary action could be taken. Treasury recovered the full value of the overpayments.

Company Forced to Repay Treasury in Full for Fraudulent 1603 Claim

A private company that provides and installs solar electrical power systems submitted to Treasury an invoice showing that it had made a $19,166 payment to a subcontractor. Based on that invoice, Treasury reimbursed the company 30 percent of its value, $5,750, in accordance with Section 1603 of the Recovery Act. The invoice showed a payment that had never been made, and the company submitted the invoice knowing that it was fraudulent, with the intent to collect funds to which it was not entitled. While the case was not accepted for criminal prosecution, Treasury compelled the company to make restitution in full, and debarment proceedings against the company are in progress.

Following is information related to significant investigative activities from prior semiannual periods.

Seven Former Bank Officers Plead Guilty to Bank Fraud

As reported in previous semiannual reports, seven officers of the First National Bank, Savannah, Georgia, were found to have subverted the OCC bank examination process by hiding millions of dollars in nonperforming loans. The subversion resulted in the bank's 2010 failure and a loss to the DIF of over $90 million.

Update: During this reporting period, the seven former bank officials pled guilty to charges of Bank Fraud, Conspiracy, Misapplication of Bank Funds, False Entries in Bank Records, and False Statements to Influence a Bank. The sentencing date has not yet been set.

Fiscal Service Employee Sentenced for Forgery

As reported in our previous semiannual report, our office substantiated an allegation that a Fiscal Service employee had created and transmitted via a Fiscal Service facsimile machine fraudulent Certificates of Insurance in an effort to help her husband obtain employment. The subject pled guilty to a state of Maryland charge of Forgery and was sentenced to 1 year of unsupervised probation and a $500 fine.

Update: During this reporting period, the employee was disciplined with a 30-day unpaid suspension.

Individual Sentenced for Felony Theft of Government Property

As reported in a previous semiannual report, the subject of this investigation was indicted on four counts of Theft in a crime involving false claims that she had never received her Social Security Administration benefit checks, then cashing both the original checks and their replacements.

Update: In this reporting period, the subject pled guilty to one charge of Felony Theft of government property and was sentenced to 4 years of probation and restitution of approximately $49,000.

Other OIG Accomplishments and Activities

CIGIE Award Ceremony

Treasury OIG staff members were recognized with four prestigious awards at the 16th Annual Council of the Inspectors General on Integrity and Efficiency (CIGIE) Awards Ceremony held on November 15, 2013.

- **June Gibbs Brown Career Achievement Award:** In recognition of **Joel Grover**, Deputy Assistant Inspector General for Financial Management and IT Audits (Retired), for his many years of exemplary service to improve federal financial management.

- **Barry R. Snyder Joint Award:** In recognition of an audit of the Financial Stability Oversight Council's Controls over Non-public Information performed by a Council of Inspectors General on Financial Oversight working group led by FDIC OIG. Treasury OIG participants on the working group were **Susan Marshall**, Executive Director, Council of Inspectors General on Financial Oversight; **Marla Freedman**, Assistant Inspector General for Audit; **Bob Taylor**, Deputy Assistant Inspector General for Audit; **Jeff Dye**, Audit Director; **Theresa Cameron**, Audit Manager; **Tim Cargill**, Auditor; **Dana Duvall**, Auditor; **Patrick Gallagher**, Auditor; and **Jen Ksanznak**, Auditor. Other working group participants honored by the award were the OIGs of the Board of Governors of the Federal Reserve System and Consumer Financial Protection Bureau, Commodity Futures Trading Commission, Federal Housing Finance Agency, National Credit Union Administration, and Securities and Exchange Commission.

- **Investigations Award for Excellence:** In recognition of **Waleska McLellan**, Special Agent, for her initiative and accomplishment in the detection and prosecution of a former Mint police officer for theft and money laundering.

- **Audit Award for Excellence:** In recognition of a first-time financial audit of the U.S. Gold Reserve Held by Federal Reserve Banks. Honored were **Mike Fitzgerald**, Audit Director; **Ade Bankole**, Audit Manager; **Rafael Cumba**, Auditor-in-Charge; **Rufus Etienne**, Senior Auditor; **Myung Han**, Audit Manager; **Robert Hong**, Auditor; **Mark Levitt**, Audit Manager; **Alicia Weber**, Auditor; and **Catherine Yi**, Audit Manager.

Keynote Speaker at CIGFO Quarterly Meeting

Harry Markopolos, author of "No One Would Listen: A True Financial Thriller", was the keynote speaker at the Council of Inspectors General on Financial Oversight's quarterly meeting on March 13, 2014. He spoke of his pursuit of Bernie Madoff's Ponzi Empire and shared his thoughts on the difficulty whistleblowers have in persuading others to take them seriously.

OIG 2013 Combined Federal Campaign Exceeds Its Goal

Treasury OIG exceeded its 2013 Combined Federal Campaign (CFC) dollar participation goal. The OIG's campaign this year was led by **John Phillips**, Assistant Inspector General for Investigations. Also assisting in the campaign were **Jennifer Ward,** Administrative Specialist, Office of Investigations, who served as the campaign coordinator; and keyworkers **Richard Delmar**, Counsel to the Inspector General; **Brigit Hoover**, Auditor, **Joshua Dreis**, Auditor, **Dionne Smith**, Auditor, and **Allison Jackson**, Program Analyst, Office of Audit; **Maria Carden**, Auditor, Office of SBLF Program Oversight; and **Chartara Floyd**, Human Resources Specialist, Office of Management.

OIG Audit Leadership Roles

Treasury OIG's audit professionals serve on various important public and private professional organizations supporting the federal and local government audit communities. Examples of participation in these organizations follow:

Marla Freedman, Assistant Inspector General for Audit, continued to serve as co-chair of the Federal Audit Executive Council's Professional Development Committee. One of the committee's activities this period was to work with the Office of Personnel Management on an initiative to address the auditor skill gap. The committee also participated in CIGIE Training Institute curriculum reviews of its auditor course offerings.

Kieu Rubb, Audit Director, led a group of interagency volunteers to update CIGIE's guide for conducting external peer reviews of federal audit organizations. During the period, a draft update to the guide was circulated to the Inspector General Community for comment. Ms. Rubb also served as an instructor for external peer review courses sponsored by the CIGIE Training Institute and the Department of Defense OIG.

Debbie Harker, Audit Director, and **Marco Uribe**, Auditor, made presentations in Montgomery, Alabama, on the Gulf Coast Ecosystem Restoration Oversight before representatives of the state of Alabama, Department of Examiners of Public Accounts during the state's 2013-2014 Annual Training Conference.

Bob Taylor, Deputy Assistant Inspector General for Audit, and **Jeff Dye**, Audit Director, taught modules of the Introductory Auditor course sponsored by the CIGIE Training Institute.

Mike Maloney, Audit Director, continued to serve on the American Institute of Certified Public Accountants' Committee on Governmental Accounting and Auditing Update Conference, and recruited five speakers for the August 2014 conference.

Statistical Summary

Summary of OIG Activity

For the 6 months ended March 31, 2014

OIG Activity	Number or Dollar Value
Office of Counsel Activity	
Regulation and legislation reviews	0
Instances where information was refused	0
Office of Audit Activities	
Reports issued and other products	36
Disputed audit recommendations	0
Significant revised management decisions	0
Management decision in which the Inspector General disagrees	0
Monetary benefits (audit)	
Questioned costs	$0
Funds put to better use	$0
Revenue enhancements	$0
Total monetary benefits	$0
Office of Small Business Lending Fund Program Oversight Activities	
Reports issued and other products	9
Disputed audit recommendations	0
Significant revised management decisions	0
Management decision in which the Inspector General disagrees	0
Monetary benefits (audit)	
Questioned costs	$49,155
Funds put to better use	$111,690
Revenue enhancements	$0
Total monetary benefits	$160,845
Office of Investigations Activities	
Criminal and judicial actions (including joint investigations)	
Cases referred for prosecution and/or litigation	29
Cases accepted for prosecution and/or litigation	12
Arrests	1
Indictments/informations	11
Convictions (by trial and plea)	22

Significant Unimplemented Recommendations

For reports issued prior to April 1, 2013

The following list of OIG audit reports with unimplemented recommendations is based on information in Treasury's automated audit recommendation tracking system, which is maintained by Treasury management officials.

Number	Date	Report Title and Recommendation Summary
OIG-06-030	05/06	*Terrorist Financing/Money Laundering: FinCEN Has Taken Steps to Better Analyze Bank Secrecy Act Data but Challenges Remain* FinCEN should enhance the current FinCEN database system or acquire a new system. An improved system should provide for complete and accurate information on the case type, status, resources, and time expended in performing the analysis. This system should also have the proper security controls to maintain integrity of the data. (1 recommendation)
OIG-11-036	11/10	*Information Technology: Treasury is Generally in Compliance with Executive Order 13103* The Chief Information Officer should (1) revise Treasury Directive 85-02 to (a) define authorized software more specifically, (b) require heads of bureaus and offices to ensure that software in their inventory is on the Treasury list of authorized software and remove it if it is not, (c) require the Chief Information Officer to perform periodic audit checks to determine if the bureaus and offices are only using software on the Treasury list of authorized software, and (d) require the bureaus and offices to reconcile their inventory with software license agreements rather than with software purchases; (2) develop procedures to create and manage a list of approved enterprise authorized software; and (3) ensure that bureaus remove unauthorized software from Treasury systems. (3 recommendations)
OIG-12-076	9/12	*Information Technology: Treasury's Security Management of TNet Needs Improvement* The Treasury Chief Information Officer should ensure that (1) security patches are implemented within 36 hours of availability in accordance with the contract; and (2) the Treasury Network (TNet) program management office, in coordination with the contracting officer and contracting officer's representative, (a) review all security performance measures in the contract, (b) negotiate with AT&T Corporation (AT&T) the terms for when penalties

are to be applied in the event a measure is not met, and (c) amend the contract accordingly. (2 recommendations)

OIG-13-034	3/13	*Information Technology: The Department of the Treasury Was Not in Compliance With the Improper Payments Elimination and Recovery Act for Fiscal Year 2012 (IPERA)* The Assistant Secretary for Management should ensure that Treasury submits a comprehensive plan to Congress that includes a description of the corrective actions Treasury will take to remediate non-compliance with IPERA due to IRS's Earned Income Tax Credit improper payments reporting deficiencies. (1 recommendation)

Summary of Instances Where an Information or Assistance Request Was Refused

October 1, 2013, through March 31, 2014

There were no instances where an information or assistance request was refused for this reporting period.

Listing of Audit Products Issued

October 1, 2013, through March 31, 2014

Office of Audit

Referral of Potential OFAC Violations By Three Banks, OIG-CA-14-001, 10/17/2013 (Sensitive But Unclassified)

Referral of Potential OFAC Violations By Three Banks, OIG-CA-14-002, 10/17/2013 (Sensitive But Unclassified)

Information Technology: OCC's Network and Systems Security Controls Were Deficient, OIG-14-001, 10/17/2013

Safety and Soundness: In-Depth Review of Second Federal Savings and Loan Association of Chicago, OIG-14-002, 10/28/2013

RESTORE Act: Gulf Coast Ecosystem Restoration Council Faces Challenges in Completing Initial Comprehensive Plan, OIG-14-003, 10/25/2013

Information Technology: The Department of the Treasury Federal Information Security Management Act Fiscal Year 2013 Evaluation for Collateral National Security Systems, OIG-CA-14-005, 11/22/2013 (Sensitive But Unclassified)

Information Technology: The Department of the Treasury Federal Information Security Management Act Fiscal Year 2013 Evaluation, OIG-CA-14-006, 11/25/2013

Audit of the United States Mint's Schedules of Custodial Deep Storage Gold and Silver Reserves as of September 30, 2013 and 2012, OIG-14-004, 11/26/2013

Report on the Bureau of the Fiscal Service Trust Fund Management Branch Schedules for Selected Trust Funds as of and for the Year Ended September 30, 2013, OIG-14-005, 12/6/2013

Audit of the Federal Financing Bank's Fiscal Years 2013 and 2012 Financial Statements, OIG-14-006, 12/11/2013

Audit of the Community Development Financial Institutions Fund's Fiscal Years 2013 and 2012 Financial Statements, OIG-14-007, 12/13/2013

Management Letter for the Audit of the Community Development Financial Institutions Fund's Fiscal Years 2013 and 2012 Financial Statements, OIG-14-008, 12/13/2013

Audit of the Exchange Stabilization Fund's Fiscal Years 2013 and 2012 Financial Statements, OIG-14-009, 12/13/2013

Audit of the Department of the Treasury Forfeiture Fund's Fiscal Years 2013 and 2012 Financial Statements, OIG-14-010, 12/16/2013

Audit of the Department of the Treasury's Fiscal Years 2013 and 2012 Financial Statements, OIG-14-011, 12/16/2013

Audit of the Department of the Treasury's Closing Package Financial Statements for Fiscal Years 2013 and 2012, OIG-14-012, 12/17/2013

Safety and Soundness: Failed Bank Review of Mountain National Bank, OIG-14-013, 12/18/2013

General Management: OCC's Leasing Activities Conformed With Applicable Requirements; Issues With the Former OTS Headquarters Building Need to Be Resolved, OIG-14-014, 12/20/2013

Audit of the United States Mint's Fiscal Years 2013 and 2012 Financial Statements, OIG-14-015, 1/13/2014

Audit of the Bureau of the Fiscal Service's Fiscal Years 2013 and 2012 Schedules of Non-Entity Government-wide Cash, OIG-14-016, 1/14/2014

Audit of the Bureau of the Fiscal Service's Fiscal Years 2013 and 2012 Schedules of Non-Entity Costs and Custodial Revenue, OIG-14-017, 1/14/2014

Management Report for the Audit of the Bureau of the Fiscal Service's Fiscal Years 2013 and 2012 Schedules of Non-Entity Government-wide Cash, OIG-14-018, 1/17/2014, (Sensitive But Unclassified)

Management Report for the Audit of the Bureau of the Fiscal Service's Fiscal Years 2013 and 2012 Schedules of Non-Entity Assets, Non-Entity Costs and Custodial Revenue, OIG-14-019, 1/17/2014, (Sensitive But Unclassified)

Management Letter for the Audit of the Department of the Treasury's Fiscal Years 2013 and 2012 Financial Statements, OIG-14-020, 1/22/2014

Audit of the Bureau of Engraving and Printing's Fiscal Years 2013 and 2012 Financial Statements, OIG-14-021, 1/27/2014

Management Letter for the Audit of the Bureau of Engraving and Printing's Fiscal Years 2013 and 2012 Financial Statements, OIG-14-022, 1/28/2014

CDFI Fund Needs Better Controls Over Travel, OIG-14-023, 1/29/2014

Audit of the Office of the Comptroller of the Currency's Fiscal Years 2013 and 2012 Financial Statements, OIG-14-024, 2/4/2014

Management Letter for the Audit of the Office of the Comptroller of the Currency's Fiscal Years 2013 and 2012 Financial Statements, OIG-14-025, 2/4/2014

Audit of the Alcohol and Tobacco Tax and Trade Bureau's Fiscal Years 2013 and 2012 Financial Statements, OIG-14-026, 2/5/2014

Audit of the Department of the Treasury's Schedules of United States Gold Reserves Held by Federal Reserve Banks as of September 30, 2013 and 2012, OIG-14-027, 2/7/2014

Recovery Act: Audit of New Mexico Mortgage Finance Authority's Payment Under 1602 Program, OIG-14-028, 3/10/2014

Peer Review of CIA, OIG-CA-14-007, 3/20/2014 (Classified)

Terrorist Financing/Money Laundering: FinCEN's BSA IT Modernization Program is on Budget, on Schedule, and Close to Completion, OIG-14-029, 3/25/2014

Transfer of Office of Thrift Supervision Functions Is Completed, OIG-14-030, 3/26/2014

Fiscal Service Needs to Improve Program Management of Direct Express, OIG-14-031, 3/26/2014

Office of SBLF Program Oversight

State Small Business Credit Initiative: Treasury Needs to Modify Its Capital-at-Risk Requirements for Capital Access Programs, OIG-SBLF-14-001, 10/24/2013

State Small Business Credit Initiative: Florida's Use of Federal Funds for Capital Access and Other Credit Support Programs, OIG-SBLF-14-002, 11/15/2013

State Small Business Credit Initiative: Louisiana's Eligibility for its Second Transfer of Funds and the Allowability of Reported Administrative Expenses, OIG-SBLF-14-003, 1/9/2014

State Small Business Credit Initiative: West Virginia's Use of Federal Funds for Other Credit Support Programs, OIG-SBLF-14-004, 3/19/2014

State Small Business Credit Initiative: Illinois' Use of Federal Funds for Capital Access and Other Credit Support Programs, OIG-SBLF-14-005, 3/26/14, **$105,000 Funds Put to Better Use**

State Small Business Credit Initiative: South Carolina's Use of Federal Funds for Capital Access and Other Credit Support Programs, OIG-SBLF-14-006, 3/26/14

State Small Business Credit Initiative: American Samoa's Administrative Expenses and Reporting, OIG-SBLF-14-007, 3/26/14, **$49,155 Questioned Cost**

Small Business Lending Fund: Survey of Small Business Lending Fund Participants on Use of Program Funds, Repayment Plans, and Satisfaction with Treasury's Program Administration, OIG-SBLF-14-008, 3/27/14

State Small Business Credit Initiative: North Carolina's Use of Federal Funds for Capital Access and Other Credit Support Programs, OIG-SBLF-14-009, 3/27/14, **$6,690 Funds Put to Better Use**

Audit Reports Issued With Questioned Costs

October 1, 2013, through March 31, 2014

Category	Total No. of Reports	Total Questioned Costs	Total Unsupported Costs
For which no management decision had been made by beginning of reporting period	3	$392,782	$0
Which were issued during the reporting period	1	$49,155	$0
Subtotals	4	$441,937	$0
For which a management decision was made during the reporting period	3	$392,782	$0
Dollar value of disallowed costs	3	$392,782	$0
Dollar value of costs not disallowed	0	$0	$0
For which no management decision was made by the end of the reporting period	1	$49,155	$0
For which no management decision was made within 6 months of issuance	0	$0	$0

Audit Reports Issued With Recommendations That Funds Be Put to Better Use

October 1, 2013, through March 31, 2014

Category	Total No. of Reports	Total	Savings	Revenue Enhancement
For which no management decision had been made by beginning of reporting period	1	$240,000	$240,000	$0
Which were issued during the reporting period	2	$111,690	$111,690	$0
Subtotals	3	$351,690	$351,690	$0
For which a management decision was made during the reporting period	1	$240,000	$240,000	$0
Dollar value of recommendations agreed to by management	1	$240,000	$240,000	$0
Dollar value based on proposed management action	1	$240,000	$240,000	$0
Dollar value based on proposed legislative action	0	$0	$0	$0
Dollar value of recommendations not agreed to by management	0	$0	$0	$0
For which no management decision was made by the end of the reporting period	2	$111,690	$111,690	$0
For which no management decision was made within 6 months of issuance	0	$0	$0	$0
A recommendation that funds be put to better use denotes funds could be used more efficiently if management took actions to implement and complete the recommendation including: (1) reduction in outlays, (2) de-obligations of funds from programs or operations, (3) costs not incurred by implementing recommended improvements related to operations, (4) avoidance of unnecessary expenditures noted in pre-award review of contract or grant agreements, (5) any other savings which are specifically identified, or (6) enhancements to revenues of the federal government.				

Previously Issued Audit Reports Pending Management Decisions (Over 6 Months)

There were no previously issued audit reports pending management decisions for the reporting period.

Significant Revised Management Decisions

October 1, 2013, through March 31, 2014

There were no significant revised management decisions during the reporting period.

Significant Disagreed Management Decisions

October 1, 2013, through March 31, 2014

There were no management decisions this reporting period with which the Inspector General was in disagreement.

Peer Reviews

October 1, 2013, through March 31, 2014

Office of Audit and Office of SBLF Program Oversight

Audit organizations that perform audits and attestation engagements of federal government programs and operations are required by *Government Auditing Standards* to undergo an external peer review every 3 years. The objectives of an external peer review are to determine, during the period under review, whether, the audit organization's system of quality control was suitably designed and whether the audit organization was complying with its quality control system to provide the audit organization with reasonable assurance that it was conforming to applicable professional standards. Federal audit organizations can receive a peer review rating of *pass, pass with deficiencies*, or *fail*.

Our Office of Audit and Office of SBLF Program Oversight were not required to undergo an external peer review during this reporting period. The most recent peer review of our offices was performed by the U.S. Agency for International Development (USAID) OIG. In its report dated September 6, 2012, our audit organizations received a *pass* rating for our system of quality control in effect for the year ended March 31, 2012. USAID OIG did not make any recommendations. Our offices' external peer review reports are available on the Treasury OIG website.

During this semiannual period, we completed an external peer review of the Central Intelligence Agency OIG's system of quality control for its audit organization in effect for the year ended September 30, 2013. In our report, dated March 20, 2014, we provided a *pass* rating on the Central Intelligence Agency OIG's system of quality control for its audit organization. We did not make any recommendations.

Office of Investigations

CIGIE mandates that the investigative law enforcement operations of all OIGs undergo peer reviews every 3 years to ensure compliance with (1) the council's investigations quality standards and with (2) the relevant guidelines established by the Office of the Attorney General of the United States.

Our Office of Investigations is currently undergoing a CIGIE peer review during this reporting period. The previous peer review of our office was performed in March 2011 by the Small Business Administration OIG. We were found to be in compliance with all relevant guidelines and there are no unaddressed recommendations outstanding from this review.

Bank Failures and Nonmaterial Loss Reviews

We conducted reviews of three failed banks supervised by OCC with losses to the DIF that did not meet the definition of a material loss in the Federal Deposit Insurance Act. These reviews were performed to fulfill the requirements found in 12 U.S.C. § 1831o(k). The term "material loss" which, in turn, triggers an MLR be performed is, for 2013, a loss to the DIF that exceeds $150 million; and, for 2014 going forward, a loss to the DIF that exceeds $50 million (with provisions to increase that trigger to a loss that exceeds $75 million under certain circumstances).

For losses that are not material, the Federal Deposit Insurance Act requires that each 6-month period, the OIG of the federal banking agency must (1) identify the estimated losses that have been incurred by the DIF during that 6-month period and (2) determine the grounds identified by the failed institution's regulator for appointing the FDIC as receiver, and whether any unusual circumstances exist that might warrant an in-depth review of the loss. For each 6-month period, we are also required to prepare a report to the failed institutions' regulator and the Congress that identifies (1) any loss that warrants an in-depth review, together with the reasons why such a review is warranted and when the review will be completed; and (2) any losses where we determine no in-depth review is warranted, together with an explanation of how we came to that determination. The table below fulfills this reporting requirement to the Congress for the 6-month period ended March 31, 2014. We issue separate audit reports on each review to OCC.

Bank Failures and Non Material Loss Reviews				
Bank Name/Location	Date Closed/ Loss to the DIF	OIG Summary of Regulator's Grounds for Receivership	In-Depth Review Determination	Reason/ Anticipated Completion Date of the In-Depth Review
Texas Community Bank, National Association The Woodlands, Texas	December 13, 2013 $10.8 million	• Dissipation of assets or earnings due to unsafe or unsound practices • Unsafe or unsound condition • Capital impaired	No	No unusual circumstances noted
DuPage National Bank West Chicago, Illinois	January 17, 2014 $1.6 million	• Dissipation of assets or earnings due to unsafe or unsound practices • Unsafe or unsound condition • Capital impaired	No	No unusual circumstances noted
Millennium Bank, National Association Sterling, Virginia	February 28, 2014 $7.7 million	• Dissipation of assets or earnings due to unsafe or unsound practices • Unsafe or unsound condition • Capital impaired	No	No unusual circumstances noted

References to the Inspector General Act

Section	Requirement	Page
Section 4(a)(2)	Review of legislation and regulations	31
Section 5(a)(1)	Significant problems, abuses, and deficiencies	5-28
Section 5(a)(2)	Recommendations with respect to significant problems, abuses, and deficiencies	5-28
Section 5(a)(3)	Significant unimplemented recommendations described in previous semiannual reports	32-33
Section 5(a)(4)	Matters referred to prosecutive authorities	31
Section 5(a)(5)	Summary of instances where information was refused	33
Section 5(a)(6)	List of audit reports	33-36
Section 5(a)(7)	Summary of significant reports	5-28
Section 5(a)(8)	Audit reports with questioned costs	37
Section 5(a)(9)	Recommendations that funds be put to better use	38
Section 5(a)(10)	Summary of audit reports issued before the beginning of the reporting period for which no management decision had been made	38
Section 5(a)(11)	Significant revised management decisions made during the reporting period	38
Section 5(a)(12)	Management decisions with which the Inspector General is in disagreement	39
Section 5(a)(13)	Instances of unresolved Federal Financial Management Improvement Act noncompliance	7
Section 5(a)(14)	Results of peer reviews conducted of Treasury OIG by another OIG	39-40
Section 5(a)(15)	List of outstanding recommendations from peer reviews	39-40
Section 5(a)(16)	List of peer reviews conducted by Treasury OIG, including a list of outstanding recommendations from those peer reviews	39-40
Section 5(d)	Serious or flagrant problems, abuses, or deficiencies	N/A
Section 6(b)(2)	Report to Secretary when information or assistance is unreasonably refused	33

Abbreviations

BSA	Bank Secrecy Act
BSA IT Mod	BSA Information Technology Modernization Program
CAP	Capital Access Program
CDFI	Community Development Financial Institutions
CFC	Combined Federal Campaign
CIGIE	Council of the Inspectors General on Integrity and Efficiency
Comerica	Comerica Bank
Council	Gulf Coast Ecosystem Restoration Council
DIF	Deposit Insurance Fund
Direct Express	Direct Express® Debit MasterCard® program
Dodd-Frank	Dodd-Frank Wall Street Reform and Consumer Protection Act of 2010
FAA	Financial Agency Agreement
FDIC	Federal Deposit Insurance Corporation
FinCEN	Financial Crimes Enforcement Network
Fiscal Service	Bureau of the Fiscal Service
FISMA	Federal Information Security Management Act
FRB	Board of Governors of the Federal Reserve System
GAO	Government Accountability Office
IPERA	Improper Payments Elimination and Recovery Act for Fiscal Year 2012
IRS	Internal Revenue Service
IT	information technology
ITIN	individual taxpayer identification numbers
Justice	U.S. Department of Justice
KPMG	KPMG LLP
MFA	New Mexico Mortgage Finance Authority
MLR	material loss review
OCC	Office of the Comptroller of the Currency
OFAC	Office of Foreign Assets Control
OIG	Office of Inspector General
OMB	Office of Management and Budget
OTS	Office of Thrift Supervision
Plan	Joint Implementation Plan
Recovery Act	American Recovery and Reinvestment Act of 2009
RESTORE Act	Resources and Ecosystems Sustainability, Tourist Opportunities, and Revived Economies of the Gulf Coast States Act of 2012
SBLF	Small Business Lending Fund
SSBCI	State Small Business Credit Initiative
TARP	Troubled Asset Relief Program
TIGTA	Treasury Inspector General for Tax Administration
USAID	U.S. Agency for International Development

The Salmon P. Chase Suite in the Treasury Building, Washington, DC

Salmon Chase served as the Secretary of the Treasury under President Lincoln from 1861 to 1864. His term of office occurred during the years of the Civil War and many of the measures undertaken in Chase's office were in response to wartime needs. To help finance the war, Secretary Chase mandated the Legal Tender Act of 1862 in which "greenback" currency was created, backed by neither silver nor gold. In response to a monetary system where states and individual banks printed their own money, a national banking system was instituted and became law in February of 1863. Also under Secretary Chase's direction, the Treasury Department oversaw the creation of two bureaus: the Bureau of Engraving and Printing which produced the new federal notes, and the Bureau of Internal Revenue (later renamed the Internal Revenue Service) which was responsible for collecting a new income tax to help finance the War. Chase resigned his position as Secretary of the Treasury in June of 1864 and was appointed Chief Justice of the United States Supreme Court in the fall of that year. He presided on the bench during the turbulent era of Reconstruction until his death in 1873.

(Source: http://www.treasury.gov/about/history/Pages/chase-suite.aspx)